The Curse of Blessings

The Curse of Blessings

SOMETIMES THE RIGHT
STORY CAN
CHANGE YOUR LIFE

by Mitchell Chefitz

RUNNING PRESS
PHILADELPHIA · LONDON

Library of Congress Control Number 9780762426775

ISBN-13: 978-0-7624-2677-5
ISBN-10: 0-7624-2677-2

Cover designed by Bill Jones
Interior designed by Corinda Cook
Illustrated by Julie Paschkis
Edited by Deborah Grandinetti
Typography: Baskerville

This book may be ordered by mail from the publisher.
Please include $2.50 for postage and handling.
But try your bookstore first!

Running Press Book Publishers
125 South Twenty-Second Street
Philadelphia, Pennsylvania 19103-4399

Visit us on the web!
www.runningpress.com

for the boys

Josh

Adam   Walter

much love

Contents

Prologue

Reuben entrusted these stories to me.

They were a parting gift. Now, they're our gift to you.

Let me share with you some of the mystery of how they came to be . . .

✦ ✦ ✦

I was one of four who gathered around Reuben in Central Park during our lunch break. Others came now and then, stayed a while, then floated away. But we four remained faithful to Reuben and each other nearly two years. He showed such a loving interest in each of us. And his insights were priceless.

All we knew of Reuben was that he commuted from New Jersey just to sit in the park, weather permitting. That was the work of his retirement.

Each of us came from some other place. One was a diamond merchant, one a social worker, one a Wall Street man, and me, an attorney. I specialize in intellectual property.

Only now that Reuben has left to be with his family in Florida do we realize how much his stories have changed us. I'm curious to see what effect they'll have on you.

✦ ✦ ✦

Shortly before he gave them to us, Reuben presented us with a puzzle.

"An old story," he said. "There was a great archer, the royal archer, the best in the land. But he was dissatisfied. He'd set his target a hundred yards away, raise his bow, and release the arrow. But as the arrow rose through the sky, it would encounter the wind. When it fell to the target, it fell less than perfect. A few inches to the right. A few to the left. A remarkable accomplishment, but less than perfect.

"Time after time, he came close, but the wind made his craft uncertain. He left the city to search for a place where there was no wind, no uncertainty, so he might practice his craft to perfection.

"As he traveled, he came upon a barn. On the side of the barn were twelve targets. Precisely in the center of each target. Precisely. 'This is a greater archer than I am,' the royal archer thought. 'I have to find him.' So he inquired. Each person told him he was not looking for an archer. He was looking for a fool. 'Perhaps a fool,' the royal archer said, 'but a great archer nonetheless.' 'You don't understand,' they told him. 'He shoots the arrow first, then he paints the targets.'"

"It's not a story. It's a joke," said our diamond merchant.

Reuben smiled his old man smile, knowing he had us

in his web. "A joke may be just a joke," he said, "or a joke may be a compressed story. There is a story here. Can you find it?"

✦ ✦ ✦

The next day we gathered around Reuben. He was sitting on the edge of his bench in eager anticipation. "What are we to do with our royal archer?" he asked.

"It's a joke," said the diamond merchant. "There isn't anything to do with it."

"It's a story," I said. I had found the royal archer in my dreams that night.

Reuben leaned forward. "Yes? Then tell me the rest of it."

✦ ✦ ✦

"The royal archer must have been angry, very angry, that someone would make such a mockery of his art," I began. "This painter needed a scolding."

"With a sword," the Wall Street man said.

"No sword," said the social worker. "Just a scolding. He found the house of the painter, pounded on the door."

"The door opened," the diamond merchant said, "and there stood a middle-aged man with a beer belly, looking up through his spectacles at the royal archer."

"Is this still a joke to you?" I asked.

The diamond merchant opened his mouth to add to the

joke, but in that moment, mouth still open, the joke turned toward a story. "The painter said, 'It's you! You're the royal archer! You're the greatest archer who has ever lived, standing here, at my house, in my doorway! I have admired you for years! I can't begin to tell you . . .' On and on the painter went. With each phrase, the anger of the royal archer diminished."

"So it's a story after all," I said.

"Maybe," said the diamond merchant. "The painter invited the royal archer to come inside for a cup of tea."

"So the royal archer entered the house," the Wall Street man continued. "What choice did he have? He sat with the painter, drank a cup of tea."

The Wall Street man had nothing to add, but the social worker did. "When the royal archer's anger had fully dissipated, he asked, 'Would you be kind enough, please, to tell me why you do what you do? Why do you shoot a dozen arrows at the barn and then paint the targets around them?' "

Reuben waited patiently for one of us to develop an answer. It was I who did so, astonished by my own words.

" 'A dozen arrows? I don't shoot a dozen arrows. I shoot a *hundred* arrows. I'm so thrilled when even one strikes the side of the barn! When I managed a dozen, that was reason to celebrate. I may not be much of an archer, but I am a painter, so

I celebrated each hit by painting the most beautiful target I could paint.' "

"Is that the story, Reuben?" the social worker asked.

"How should I know? It's *your* story."

"There's more," said the diamond merchant.

"More?" asked Reuben.

"I don't know," said the diamond merchant. "But that's not the end of the story."

✦ ✦ ✦

After was a long pause, Reuben picked up the thread. "The archer was looking for certainty, and all he found was a painter."

"There is no certainty in the wind," the Wall Street man said, "and there is no place without wind." He said his words with conviction, but not direction. They trailed off into silence.

Then the diamond merchant spoke: "The royal archer spent the night with the painter.

Early in the morning they both left the house with bows in hand."

"And a box of paints." The social worker was the first to see the end of the story. "They walked until they found a barn and stood a hundred yards away."

"The painter strung his bow, fitted an arrow, prepared to shoot, but the royal archer stopped him." The Wall Street man spoke with conviction *and* direction. "He showed him where to put his forward foot, how to hold the arrow . . ."

"How to focus on the target," the social worker added. "To meditate on the target, let the target attract the arrow."

"The painter released the arrow," the Wall Street man continued. "It rose into the air, descended in a graceful ark, and struck the barn."

"Way off to one side," the diamond merchant said.

"But still the painter was overjoyed." The social worker glowed with imagined pleasure.

"Then the royal archer strung his bow," the Wall Street man said. "There was a tiny dot in the center of the barn. That became his target. He pulled back the arrow. He meditated on the target, released the arrow. It rose into the sky, fell toward the target and . . ."

"Missed a few inches to the left," I said. I, too, knew the ending.

"I was going to say to the right."

"Either way. Just to be sure it missed."

"I was going to have it miss. You needn't have worried."

"The royal archer was distraught." I continued. "He had traveled so far, accomplished so little. The wind had followed him. He said, 'Were it not for the wind, it would have been a perfect hit.' "

The diamond merchant said, "But it was a perfect hit. The painter knew it. He and the royal archer approached the barn, and the painter taught the royal archer how to paint a perfect target."

Reuben waited to see if any of us had more to add. "*That's a story,*" he said. "Thank you."

✦ ✦ ✦

The next day Reuben told us he was leaving for Florida. He would be gone two weeks. His Florida family thought he would do better there.

"They must think I'm doing badly," he said. "Do you think I'm doing badly?" We surely did not. "But for two weeks I'll go."

Two weeks later he was on his bench. We were thrilled to see him. He had an old leather briefcase between his knees.

"When I was in Florida these last weeks I went inside and found you there, each of you. And with each of you I went to

15

the place where stories come from. You know where that is. It's where the royal archer is. And the painter. But most of all, it's where the wind is. The wind that keeps us from finding certainty."

From his briefcase he withdrew four packets of papers. "One for each of you."

I raised my packet to the vertical. "These stories, they're about us?"

"Not exactly," he said. "They're from within us. From around us. They flow across boundaries of space and time. They're from where we were, where we are, where we are yet to be. You'll take care of them for me, won't you?"

✦ ✦ ✦

Reuben is still with his family in Florida. With the publication of this collection I have fulfilled my obligation. I have taken care of his stories. And they have taken care of me.

They are your stories, now.

You are the target.

May they hit their mark.

The Curse of Blessings

There was an Officer of the Law, a recent graduate, proud as you can imagine, in his uniform of blue with brass buttons and gold epaulets. He wore a hat with a plume and a sword with a gold and ivory handle. He was as pompous as could be. He was arrogant and bold and callous. Every letter of the alphabet served only to demonstrate his authority and exalt his being.

One day he was walking his beat and heard a commotion in an alley. He ventured into the darkness, and there in the distance saw a man in rags. "Come forward," he commanded. "Come forward now!" But the man in rags did not come forward. "I am an Officer of the Law, and I command you, come forward!"

The man in rags did not move. He shifted his weight from one foot to the other and spoke, "I don't know what I'm going to do with you."

"Do with me?" the Officer of the Law mocked. "Do with me? You don't do with me! I do with you! I am an Officer of the Law, and I command you to come forward."

"Now I know what to do with you," the man in rags said, and as he spoke, he drew his sword. "Now I know what to do." Without further word he moved to attack.

The Officer of the Law drew his own sword in defense. "Stop that!" he ordered. "Put your sword down right now!" But the man in rags did not stop. The Officer of the Law had to parry thrusts left and right. "Stop!" he said again, but to no avail. The Officer of the Law was forced to retreat.

When it seemed the man in rags would prevail, he lowered his guard, and what the Officer of the Law had intended as a parry became a thrust. His sword ran through the man in rags. "I didn't mean that," the Officer of the Law said. "I didn't mean to hurt you. Why didn't you stop when I ordered you to? Why did you attack me?"

The man in rags waved the words away. "I am leaving you," he said, "and as I do, I put upon you the Curse of Blessings."

"What do you mean?" asked the Officer of the Law, now quite confused.

"The Curse of Blessings. Every day you must say a new blessing, one you have never said before. On the day you do not say a new blessing, on that day you will die."

The man in rags closed his eyes. The Officer of the Law looked about for help. There was none to be found. When he turned back, the man in rags had disappeared. He was gone.

"It was a dream," the Officer of the Law thought. "Only a dream. I imagined it."

The time was late in the afternoon. The sun was setting. As much as the Officer of the Law tried to ignore his experience, he could not. The Jewish day ends with the sunset. The Officer of the Law felt his body growing cold and knew from the chill that his life was leaving him. In a panic, he uttered these words of blessing: "You are blessed, Lord our God, ruler of the universe, who has created such a beautiful sunset." At once warmth and life flowed back into him. He realized, with both shock and relief, the curse had been for real.

The next morning he did not delay. He woke with words of blessing. "You are blessed that You allowed me to wake up this morning." His life felt secure the entire day. The next morning he blessed his ability to rise from his bed, the following day, that he could tie his shoes.

Day after day he found abilities he could bless. That he could go to the bathroom, that he had teeth to brush, that each finger of his hands still worked, that he had toes on his feet and hair on his head. He blessed his clothes, every garment. He blessed his house, the roof and floor, his furniture, every table and chair.

At last he ran out of things to bless, so he began to bless relationships. He blessed his family and friends, fellow workers, and those who worked for him. He blessed the mailman and the clerks. He was surprised to find they appreciated the

21

blessings. His words had power. They drew family and friends closer to him. Word went out that the Officer of the Law was a source of blessing.

Years passed, decades. The Officer of the Law had to go farther afield to find new sources of blessing. He blessed city councils and university buildings, scientists, and their discoveries. As he traveled through the world he became in awe of its balance and beauty and blessed that. The more he learned, the more he had to bless. His life was long, and he had the opportunity to learn in every field.

He passed the age of one hundred. Most of his friends were long gone. His time was relegated to searching for the purpose in his life and the one source from which all blessings flow. He had long since realized he was not the source but only the conduit, and even that realization was welcomed with a blessing that sustained him for yet another day.

As he approached the age of one hundred and twenty, he considered that his life was long enough. Even Moses had not lived longer. On his birthday he made a conscious decision to utter no new blessing and allow his life to come to an end. Still he could recite old blessings, and throughout the day he reviewed them, all the blessings for his body and his possessions, for relationships that spread throughout the world, for the awesome beauty and balance of creation, and for the deep resonance, the pulse of purpose that pervaded his very being. But no new blessing passed his lips.

As the sun was setting, a chill progressed inward from his extremities. He did not resist it. In the twilight a figure appeared, the man in rags. "You!" the Officer of the Law exclaimed. "I have thought about you every day for a hundred years! I never meant to harm you. Please, forgive me."

"You don't understand," said the man in rags. "You don't know who I am, do you? I am the angel who was sent a hundred years ago to harvest your soul, but when I looked at you, so pompous and proud, there was nothing there to harvest. An empty uniform was all I saw. So I put upon you the Curse of Blessings, and now look what you've become!"

The Officer of the Law grasped in an instant all that had happened and why. Overwhelmed he said, "You are blessed, my God, ruler of the universe, that You have kept me alive and sustained me so I could attain this moment."

"Now look what you've done!" the man in rags said in frustration. "A new blessing!"

Life flowed back into the Officer of the Law, and he and the man in rags looked to each other, neither of them knowing quite what to do.

The Wise Man Who Became Angry

. . . The wise man sensed he had once been angry. He couldn't remember quite why he had been angry. That he couldn't remember made him angrier still. His anger became so great, his wisdom departed. He became an ordinary man.

As an ordinary man he stood upright. He walked. He talked. But he remembered he had been wise. That he was no longer wise made him angry, so angry he ceased to be a man. He became an animal that walked on all fours.

As an animal he prowled the forest. His belly swung close to the earth. Once he had stood upright. He had walked and talked. Now he could only growl his discontent. His growling was such, he ceased to be an animal. He became a vine that climbed a tree.

As a vine it climbed and climbed, wrapping itself around trunk and branches, reaching toward the canopy of the forest. Even as it climbed, it knew once it had the freedom to roam between the trees. The vine chafed at its limitations. It ceased to be a vine. It became a plant, fixed in the ground.

As a plant it sent roots into the earth and stretched upward toward the light. As it flowered, it felt only regret it could no longer climb to the highest heights. Indignant at being stuck in the dirt, it ceased to be a plant and became a boulder.

As a boulder it sat with weight and integrity, solid and substantial. But resentment that it could no longer grow toward the light dwelled at its core. Only the resentment grew, swelling and swelling until the boulder shattered. The boulder became pebbles.

As pebbles, it became unsettled by every rain, rearranged by every storm. Though smoothed and polished by water and wind, the pebbles no longer had the integrity of a single entity. Dissatisfaction wore the pebbles down to dust.

As dust it experienced nothing.

A wind lifted the dust into the atmosphere, beyond the atmosphere, into the expanse of the galaxy, into the depth of the universe. The dust floated without awareness for the longest time.

At last the dust settled to earth and became pebbles. Rain and wind polished the pebbles to perfection. Pleasure fused the pebbles into a boulder.

The boulder cherished its integrity. So grateful to be solid and substantial, it opened to the light. The boulder became a plant.

The plant sipped nourishment deep from the earth, reached high toward the sun. Rejoicing in its growth, the plant flowered and became a vine.

The vine embraced a tree, circling in delight. Happiness flowed from its highest point down to the ground. The vine became an animal walking on all fours.

The animal pranced and danced through the trees, so glad for the grace of movement. It stood upright to walk and found it could talk.

The man standing upright marveled at each of his limbs. In awe of every movement, he raised his voice in praise of such wonder. The man became wise.

The wise man became one with all about him—with all men and women, with all animals, with climbing vines, flowering plants, boulders, pebbles, dust, and the nothingness beneath the dust, but . . .

. . . The wise man sensed he had once been angry. He couldn't remember quite why.

Polished Stones

A teller of fortunes, bereft of family, moved from fair to fair. Through clients' eyes he sampled despair. His words conveyed honesty, not hope, so he made no friends, found no community to anchor him from time to place.

The fortuneteller paid little attention to vendors about him, hawkers of remedies and charms. But one vendor gained his notice, an old peddler of stones, so busy with clients he had little need to hawk his wares. All about vendors proclaimed the virtues of their elixirs and trinkets, but the old peddler did little more than strew his stones upon a cloth. White, pink, blue; brilliant and pale, stones polished to perfection. The peddler kissed each stone before placing it into a client's hand.

"I see you watching me," the peddler said. "I've been watching you, too. You seem to tell the truth. Tell my fortune, I'll give you a stone." He spread a handful of gems before the teller. Agates: green specks peeking through a field of white. Amethysts: purple, bursting and blush. Aquamarines: wavelets captured from the ocean.

"Beautiful stones," the fortuneteller said. A golden beryl winked toward him. "For this I'll tell your fortune."

"Done," the peddler said. He kissed the yellow cat's eye, placed it in the teller's hand.

Ignoring the tingling in his hand the fortuneteller looked deep into the peddler's moonstone eyes.

The fortuneteller blinked, then blinked again. He saw stars and planets, galaxies turning.

"I see no fortune," he said. "No fortune at all. I can't take your stone."

"The stone is yours," the peddler said. "What you tell is honest. I have no fortune that you can see. You've earned the stone. My best to you."

The fair ended. The vendors packed their wares, each to go their separate ways.

At the next fair the teller of fortunes found the peddler once again. "Twice now I've seen you, but not before."

"We've been traveling different circles," the peddler said. "My path now seems linked to yours."

The peddler sold stones; the teller told fortunes. From the peddler each client left with a smile; from the fortuneteller each client left in despair.

"A good fair," the peddler said when the time came to move on. "Perhaps you would like another stone?"

"What do I have to offer in return?" the fortuneteller asked.

"My fortune."

"Last I looked, I saw none."

"Last time it was not there for you to see. Perhaps this time. Choose a stone."

The peddler spread his stones before the fortuneteller. Chalcedony: milky blue. Citrine: sunshine yellow. Emerald: pulsing veins of green. But it was a garnet, a deep red teardrop, that held the eyes of the fortuneteller.

"It's yours," said the peddler, kissing it and placing it in the fortuneteller's hand. "What do you see?"

The tingling in the fortune teller's hand spread through his arm to become a tremor in his shoulder, a sensation he set aside to peer into the moonstone eyes, through stars and galaxies and beyond, but he had no words for what he saw. "A mystery is all," he said.

"A mystery," the peddler repeated. "Well worth the stone. My thanks to you."

They packed their wares, each prepared to go his way.

"Perhaps travel with me," the peddler said. "We're likely on the same path."

There was room in the peddler's wagon. More than room, there was company. It had been long since the fortuneteller had company. "You're both generous and kind," he said. "Generous and kind."

They rode together at a steady pace, the steady sound of

donkey's hooves before the wagon, a soft cacophony behind. "That murmuring within the wagon," the fortuneteller said. "What is it?"

The peddler sighed. "The woes of the world, my friend. The woes of the world. How long have you been traveling?"

"Two years, now. Two years since my family died." The fortuneteller had no intent to say so much. He would say no more.

A long time they rode in silence, the sound of the donkey's hooves diminishing beneath the grinding and groans emanating from the wagon.

"Such noise back there," the fortuneteller said. "What's causing it?"

"The woes of the world, my friend. How did you lose your family?"

"In a fire. I was a broker of land, had a wonderful house." In two years he had never spoken of it. "My wife, my son, my daughter. I traveled to close a deal." He would say no more. "I returned to find my house ablaze, my family trapped within."

They continued in silence, camped in silence, each to his own side of the fire. The next day they reached the fair grounds, set up booths side by side.

The peddler sold jade. Some green, some brown, some white. "The stone of mystery!" he said.

The fortuneteller saw pain, suffering, and spoke the truth.

The peddler sold opals, sparkling with fire, "A stone for the heart!" he said.

The fortuneteller saw antagonism, conflict, failure.

The peddler sold peridot, green because it absorbed all envy. "A stone to bring comfort!" he said.

The fortuneteller saw corruption, neglect, oppression.

"It's been a good fair," the peddler said as he packed his booth. "I'll give you a stone for my future. Perhaps you will see more this time."

"Why should I see more this time than last? Why should you lose a stone?"

"I cannot lose a stone. I can only give it away. Which will you take?"

The peddler spread quartz, sapphire, and topaz before the fortuneteller. Strawberry, cobalt blue, the blue of the sky . . . But it was a green tourmaline with striations of anguish that held the teller.

"It is yours," the peddler said. He kissed the tourmaline and placed it in the fortuneteller's hand. "Now, what is my future?"

Tingling became a tremor, the tremor a shudder. The fortuneteller clenched his fists to steady himself, then gazed into the moonstone eyes. He saw beyond the stars and turning galaxies to the mystery, and through the mystery, a light too bright to penetrate. "I see no future, only the present," was all he could say.

"Such a gift you have, to speak the truth. Well worth the stone. Shall we ride together to the next fair?"

They rode together. The hooves of the donkey were barely audible against the grinding that emerged from within the wagon.

"What makes that awful sound?" the fortuneteller asked.

"The woes of the world, my friend. How did you come to be a teller of fortunes from being a broker of land?"

"The loss of my family opened my eyes. Before I could see only happiness. At weddings I used to rejoice for the bride and the groom. But after the loss of my family, I saw not only the happiness, but the pain and sorrow. I saw one dying first and the broken heart of the other.

"It used to be when a child was born I would rejoice. But after the loss of my family, I saw not only the joy the child would give, but also the heartbreak.

"No longer could I see only the happiness. I saw the other side as well, and what I saw was what would be. I saw the truth. So I went on the road to speak the truth. My friend, it's easier to sell your stones than speak the truth. You get repeat customers. I do not."

The fortuneteller heard his own words. In two years he had not called anyone a friend. Did he really have a friend?

The peddler chose a left turn instead of a right.

"The fair is the other way," the fortuneteller said.

"We have a stop to make first," the peddler said.

The wagon climbed into the hills and into the night. Dark as it was, the peddler did not stop. Stars and galaxies turned in the sky above. Such a mystery, the teller thought. Where were they going?

"Here," the peddler said, answering the unspoken question.

He stopped the wagon, lit a lantern, drew the cover back from the wagon bed. Within was machinery the likes of which the fortuneteller had never seen, a contraption turned by the power of the wagon wheels to do some work within a closed box. The peddler opened the box, removed polished stones, each glowing its unique color in the lantern light. He added them to his inventory, one at a time, each with a kiss and a thank you. "Thank you," he said to the agate. "Thank you," he said to the amethyst. "Thank you," he said to the aquamarine.

When the box was empty, his inventory full, he handed the fortuneteller a shovel and took a strainer for himself.

"What are we doing?" the fortuneteller asked.

"What is necessary," the peddler said. He walked to the side of a hill, held out the strainer and motioned to the fortuneteller. The teller drove his shovel into the side of the hill, the grating of metal against rock echoing into the distance. He struck again and again. Sand and earth sifted through the strainer leaving behind an assemblage of jagged rocks.

"What are these?" the fortuneteller asked.

"These are beryl and chalcedony. Citrine and emerald. Garnet and jade. All the precious stones of the world. All exist everywhere at all times if you just know how to look."

"All I see is rocks."

"You are a teller of fortunes," the peddler said. "Look more closely and see again."

The fortuneteller looked into the rocks and saw—buried within—moonstones. And opals. And turquoise. He saw the tumbling each would endure to allow its beauty to shine. He saw that some would shatter and never emerge, but others would be polished to perfection.

"A stone for my fortune," the peddler said. In his hand was a zircon, pulsing in the lantern light.

"Why should I be able to see a fortune where I never saw one before?" the teller asked.

"Because you've tumbled to this place," the peddler answered. He kissed the zircon, placed it into the fortuneteller's hand.

Tingling became a tremor, the tremor a shudder, and the shudder an impulse that removed all veils from the teller's sight.

The fortuneteller held the lantern, peered into peddler's moonstone eyes. He saw stars and galaxies turning, such a mystery. Behind the mystery, a light. Within the light, a man once in pain, a man who had lost his own family decades before. A man who ever after knew the truth and wandered from place to place until he encountered his own vendor of precious stones.

The fortuneteller looked into the eyes of a man who had risen from despair to beauty and hope.

"Yes, you see," the peddler said. "I've been waiting for you quite some time. Quite some time. Thank you for receiving my stones. They and the wagon are yours." The peddler smiled as he surrendered his burden.

The fortuneteller saw his friend buckle at the knees. He reached for him, embraced him, kissed him as his life expired.

The fortuneteller cried for his friend. He cried for his family. He cried for the woes of the world.

He buried his friend by the side of the hill. The rough rocks he put into the box in the wagon bed. As he drove on, he heard tumbling behind him all the woes of the world. Ahead was the fair and customers waiting for polished stones, each stone to be given with a kiss and words of comfort.

Gabriel's Horn

Gabriel celebrated his seventh birthday with family and friends. The presents he received from friends he didn't really want, but even at seven he was kind enough to appreciate each, to value the giver if not the gift.

From aunts and uncles he received dollars and cents, seven dollars and seven cents altogether. What could he do with seven dollars and seven cents?

A knock at the door, a man selling horns. "I have horns to sell and horns to trade. One to make you strong. One to make you pleasing. One to make you wise. One to draw you out of the world."

Now it wasn't for Gabriel to open the door, but he had. And it wasn't for Gabriel to talk to strangers.

"How much is a horn?" Gabriel asked, not that he wanted one, but curious enough to break a rule.

"Seven dollars and seven cents," the man said.

Gabriel thought on that. "If I had eight dollars and eight cents, how much would a horn be?"

The man laughed. "You understand much for a child so young. If you had eight dollars and eight cents the cost of a horn would be eight dollars and eight cents."

"It's good then that I have just what I have," Gabriel said.

"It's always good to have just what you have. What I have are horns to sell and horns to trade. One to make you strong. One to make you pleasing. One to make you wise. One to draw you out of the world."

Gabriel didn't want a horn, but what else would he do with seven dollars and seven cents? "One to make me strong," he said.

"Done." The man reached into his case and withdrew a shiny horn. "One to make you strong." He pocketed Gabriel's seven dollars and seven cents.

Gabriel did not try the horn at once. He waited till everyone was gone. Then, alone in his room, he put the horn to his lips, and blew enough, he thought, to make a quiet sound, but made no sound at all. He blew again, harder and harder, but still no sound. He set the horn aside.

The next day he tried again, blowing until he was purple. Nothing. He tried different angles against his lips. No sound at all. "Serves me right." But he did not throw the horn away.

The next day, and the next day, too. Air passed through, a steady whoosh, but air was all. No bugle call. No trumpet blast. But the flow of air seemed close to sound, so close.

Days passed to weeks, and weeks to months. The steady

blowing expanded his chest, straightened his back, strengthened his arms. The whoosh of air became a moan. The moan a growl. The growl a groan. The groan a sound.

"What was that sound?" his mother asked.

"Just a horn," Gabriel said. "A horn I'm learning to play."

Each day the sound came easier. One sound, then two. Two sounds, then three.

Each day Gabriel became stronger until he was strong enough and put the horn away.

✦ ✦ ✦

Gabriel was an athlete, revered in track and field. "He runs like wind," all said who watched him. "Like the very wind itself."

Turning seventeen he had no party, just a cake with candles to blow out. A single breath was all it took.

A knock at the door. The man selling horns. "I have horns to sell and horns to trade," he said. "One to make you strong. One to make you pleasing. One to make you wise. One to draw you out of the world."

"I remember you," Gabriel said. "You haven't changed at all."

"But you have changed," the man said. "You've grown up quite nicely. Well, what will you do? I have horns to sell and horns to trade."

"How much to buy a horn?"

"More than you have to spend."

"Then why offer to sell at all?"

"Such a smart young man. Why do you think?"

"So I would ask the question."

"And?"

"And learn how precious your horns are."

"They are precious indeed. You can no longer buy one. But you can trade. I have one to make you strong. One to make you pleasing. One to make you wise. One to draw you out of the world."

"I've had the one to make me strong long enough," Gabriel said. "I'll trade for the one to make me pleasing."

Before returning his childhood horn Gabriel sounded one last blast that rattled windows blocks away.

"Impressive," said the man, clearly not impressed at all. "Let's see how you do with this." He presented Gabriel a silver trumpet, mirror bright inside and out.

Gabriel didn't try the horn at once. He thought to wait to after dinner. After dinner, to the next day. The next day, to the next evening. He knew how difficult a new horn might be.

At last he lifted the silver mouthpiece to his lips. Just the slightest breath produced a sound, so soft, so sweet. The trumpet sang one note, then another.

"Where is that coming from?" his mother asked.

"From this," Gabriel said.

"I didn't know you could play the trumpet."

"Nor did I."

But he could play. People came to hear, a few at first, then many. Such a sweet tone. Such a pleasing young man.

In due time the man was married.

Through the years he wondered if it was he who played the trumpet, or the trumpet that played him. He set the silver horn aside to try another instrument. The tone was different, the sound just fine. Soon the shape and size of the horn mattered little. The silver horn he put away against such a day he might need it, but through many years he never did. From time to time he would take it out to look at it. Mirror bright inside and out.

Never did it need polishing. Never did it a collect a fingerprint.

"Not mine," he understood at last. He kept it safe, a loan until the seller of horns might return.

His twenty-seventh birthday had come and gone without a knock at the door. His thirty-seventh as well. By the time he was forty-seven, he had forgotten the seller of horns, content and satisfied with his family and friends.

✦ ✦ ✦

On his forty-seventh birthday, a knock at the door. The man selling horns. "I have horns to sell and horns to trade," he said. "One to make you strong. One to make you pleasing. One to make you wise. One to draw you out of the world."

"I expected to see you years ago," Gabriel said when he caught his breath from the surprise.

"You couldn't see me then because your expectations were so great. Now that you don't expect me, here I am. I have horns to sell and horns to trade. What will you do?"

"I'll trade. I have a horn I have been keeping for you."

Gabriel retrieved the silver trumpet and was tempted to play a last trill of notes, but refrained. "I'll trade for the one to make me wise."

"Done," said the seller of horns. From his case he withdrew a simple, straight golden horn. "But with this comes a task." He turned the horn so Gabriel could look into the mouth of it. The outside of the horn was golden and opaque, but inside the horn was translucent like glass. "Your task is to paint the inside of the horn. Do you agree?"

Not difficult to do, Gabriel thought. Simply fill the horn with paint and pour the paint out. "I agree," he said.

He took the horn but nearly dropped it. It was light and heavy at the same time.

"Let me know when you would like to see me again," the seller of horns said.

"How do I reach you?"

"You expect me to tell you? Such expectations! You are holding a horn to make you wise. You figure it out."

The man turned his back. Gabriel closed the door.

What manner of horn did he have? He thought to make a sound, but his new horn was closed at the end, no opening whatsoever through which to blow.

Opaque on the outside, clear from the inside. He resolved to solve the puzzle quickly with a quart of blue paint. Just enough, he thought. He held the horn upright, filled the horn with paint to the top of its mouth, then emptied the paint back into the can.

Opaque on the outside, still clear on the inside. No change. Gabriel was puzzled by that, still more puzzled by the paint in the can. The can held only half as much as he had poured. Where had the rest of the paint gone?

The half that remained he poured into the horn, then back into the can. No change in the horn, but the can held only half again what he had poured. Back and forth, from can to horn, from horn to can. The horn remained the same but the paint diminished until there was not enough left to pour.

This was more than he could handle alone.

The paint store man said the color was the problem. "Not blue with gold. Try green. Or pink."

No matter the color, the result was the same. It was not a

matter of the quality of paint, but the quantity.

A friend who read science magazines made measurements. "The horn consumes half, and then half again, but never all. It's as if you were speeding toward a wall, covered half the distance and then half again. No matter how close, half will always be left, and so you will never hit the wall."

Not true, Gabriel knew. But why not true required some time to learn. He learned, but the learning didn't solve the puzzle.

He sought better advice at a college. A mathematician explained the volume of such a horn might be finite, but the internal surface area infinite. He wrote the formulae for him to see. Gabriel learned the calculus, understood the statements, but none could explain the horn and the paint.

"You're not the first to imagine such a horn," the professors told him. "Evangelista Torricelli did so before you, but he only imagined it."

Torricelli may have imagined it, but Gabriel held the horn in his hands.

Historians taught him Torricelli had been a student of Galileo, so he learned the physics of Galileo, and the physics before Galileo.

For years he learned.

Chemistry, mathematics, physics.

Cosmology, relativity, string theory.

Such appreciation he gained. Wisdom, he learned, was to appreciate. To resonate to beauty both small and large.

Fifty-seven, sixty-seven, seventy-seven, eighty. He learned half of everything there was to know, then half again. Eighty-seven, ninety.

Ninety-seven. He held the horn in his hands, a wonder, a marvel. Gold on the outside, clear on the inside. Closed at the bottom.

But where did the paint go? Where had the paint gone?

With a flash and a rush he knew.

He held the horn to his mouth, the tip embraced by his lips. Even a breath would be too much. He sighed a sigh through the aperture. It went, as he knew it would, in a steady stream into the horn, and painted it. When every square inch was covered with his soul, the horn proclaimed much more than a sound. It proclaimed understanding and redemption. Love and acceptance. Grace and beauty.

"You reached me," said the seller of horns. "I have horns to sell and horns to trade. One to make you strong. One to make you pleasing. One to make you wise. One to draw you out of the world. What would you like to do?"

"I'm happy to see you," Gabriel said. "I'm ready." He held out the horn that had made him wise. "If you would be so kind, I would like to trade up."

Mouth of the Mountain

As a child Stoner trembled at the whispered stories. As an adult he knew their purpose—to keep children in line. So he, in turn, whispered the stories to his own children as soon as they were old enough to tremble.

"The village walls are to keep monsters out," he said. "Monsters to the left and monsters to the right.

"Left-side monsters are green, each with three eyes, and horns as sharp as a stonecutter's tool. They rip children open from the belly up, then eat them from the inside out.

"Right-side monsters are brown, covered with bristles. They spit acid and boil children into pudding, then suck them up through funnel mouths."

Such were the stories.

Children learned not to venture to the left of the village or to the right, if they dared venture out at all.

The village sat at the base of a mountain. Throughout all recorded history, there were only two directions of travel—away from the mountain to till the fields, or up the mountain to cut the stone. No one ventured around the base of the mountain, so strong was tradition, so set the taboo.

But they did venture out to the fields to harvest crops, for villagers had to eat. And they did venture up the mountain to harvest stone, for village walls had to grow. Should the walls cease to grow, the village would cease to be.

Such was tradition.

✦ ✦ ✦

All his life Stoner had accepted tradition without question. The echoes he was hearing on the mountain gave him question, so he told the stories again, this time to grandchildren.

"Monsters to the left, and monsters to the right."

The grandchildren trembled, but Stoner paid more attention to the effect the words had upon him. He weighed and tested each spoken word as if it were a stone. Did it have proper measure? Proper finish? Proper taste? Proper soul?

Did the word of a story have the value of a stone?

Around his neck, on a rawhide chain, Stoner had suspended a polished stone cut to the sacred measure, three by two by one. The stone had value. Did the word of a story? Did the weight of an idea?

As a young apprentice, Stoner had followed his father up the mountain, carrying with him the stories of his childhood and, with the stories, his fears as well. But his father seemed not to be afraid. So Stoner followed in his father's footsteps and left his fears behind. His father's footsteps never ventured to the left or to the right, only up the mountain following veins of mica and quartz to harvest the stone, ever finer stone to meet the needs of the village below.

The first stones had been taken from the base of the mountain. Historians had cut a trench by the distal village wall. One could descend a ladder, through generations of stone, layer by layer, to see and marvel at what the ancestors had done. They must have been giants! Such massive stones! Each cut to the sacred measure. Such a mystery how they had been quarried and moved by men so primitive.

On holy days Stoner made his pilgrimage to the foundation to caress the rough surfaces. By touch and taste he could sense the soul of each stone and know from where on the mountain it had come. The higher the wall, the smaller the stone, the finer it was. Over the years, size had surrendered to quality.

Stoner's work carried him high on the mountainside, one generation above where his father had worked. So it had been since the beginning of time, each Stoner generation working above the last, each passing wisdom to the next. "Go not to the right, go not to the left, go no higher than you can cut." That was the wisdom.

It was a twelve-day climb, not venturing left or right more than a village-width, to where Stoner's team cut to the sacred measure of three by two by one.

"And what happens when we come to the top?" he asked in the camp when he was still an apprentice.

"When we come to the top our work will be done. Light will shine. Darkness will cease. When we come to the top."

Each apprentice asked the question. Each received the same answer. Light would shine, time would end when they came to the top.

They would never come to the top. Time would never come to an end. Apprentices would ask forever and receive forever the same answer.

Everything continued as it always had. Just the stone became smaller and finer.

And the echoes became louder.

"Echoes," his father answered when he asked about the distant sounds of hammers and saws. "The mountain captures the sounds we make and returns them to us whenever it chooses."

But years after his father was gone, Stoner climbed higher to find a new vein worthy of cutting. The echoes seemed louder. Louder and louder. Echoes from the left. Echoes from the right. Hammers and saws, striking and cutting. Captured sounds returned from the mountain.

"The echoes seem louder," he said in the camp.

Most of the men had learned not to hear the echoes at all.

Some said, "Just echoes. The mouth of the mountain captures our sounds and speaks them whenever it wants."

✦   ✦   ✦

With each stay in the village, after the presentation of holy stone to the Masons who set it with proper ceremony into the wall, Stoner told his grandchildren the stories. When his grandchildren tired of hearing them, he found others to tell. "Monsters to the left. Monsters to the right." He weighed and tasted every spoken word.

With each return to the camp in the mountains, he listened to the echoes. They came only by day when the mountain was awake. The mountain never echoed at night.

At the height of one ascent, the echo of a ringing hammer was so sharp, so solid, it seemed to have weight and taste. It came from the left, not from up or down.

"Monsters to the left" was a tale to frighten children. But Stoner was less certain about the mouth of the mountain from which the echoes came, and still less certain about what to do. He had no one above to consult or to ask.

Heart pounding, he stepped to the left, then to the left again, beyond a village-width, so careful with each step lest he fall into the mouth of the mountain.

He saw not a mouth, but a shadow.

"Monster," he whispered, afraid to look up.

The monster whispered back, not something intelligible. But this was not a monster, not green with three eyes. It was a man with but two eyes who seemed as amazed as Stoner was.

"Who are you?" Stoner asked, but could not understand the answer.

In the man's hand a hammer, much like the hammer Stoner held. A small hammer, sharpened at one end to probe for veins of mica and quartz.

The man struck his hammer into the mountain. This was the echo Stoner knew. Stoner struck with his hammer, a similar ring.

The mountain spoke its echoes until Stoner and the other had said enough.

The other motioned for Stoner to follow. Farther left? Did Stoner dare?

He followed to a camp of others who were cutting and polishing stone. The stone was familiar, but the shape was wrong. Too square, too thin.

Stoner reached out his hand, paused for permission,

caressed the stone. He put his fingers to his mouth to taste. The stone had soul. Too square, too thin. But fine.

For a long while he and the others sat beyond words. With the tip of his hammer, Stoner etched the sacred measure into the rock surface. Three by two by one. He pointed to the too-square stone, then to his drawing.

When they seemed not to understand, from around his neck he removed the stone he wore on a rawhide chain, handed it to the others to examine. They smelled, touched, tasted. They seemed to know its soul and returned it with respect.

Back in his camp, Stoner spoke not a word of what he had learned.

The next day, he climbed high again and ventured to the right, anticipating what he would find. No bristle-skinned brown monster, but another, like him, with a hammer, and a stone quite different, four-sided, but angular.

Days passed, camp meeting camp, stone meeting stone, a twelve-day climb above three differently walled villages at the base of the mountain.

There was one direction yet to go.

With common intent, three men climbed to the top of the mountain. Three men sat with stones, each different from the other, but each with soul the other could not deny.

Stoner said, "When we come to the top our work will be done. Light will shine. Darkness will cease. When we come to the top."

Each of the others said the same in his way.

Stoner did not know the meaning of their words, but knew the message. "Light will shine. Darkness will cease." Yet here he was, there they were, at the top of the mountain.

How was light to shine? How was darkness to cease?

They looked at each other with the question, and, with a rush of light, each had the answer.

They exchanged stones, each to bring a new understanding to his village below. Then another understanding, and another, not that holy walls would come down, but that men, women, even children, might have the courage to venture from the villages, left and right, until the circle around the mountain would be complete.

The Miku-*bal* in New Jersey

There was once a miku-*bal* who was the head of a school in Brooklyn. A miku-*bal* is a kabbalist. A kabbalist is a person who has mastered the foundation texts of Jewish tradition—the Bible, the Talmud, and the Zohar (in that order)—and who has learned how to understand those texts on the narrative, metaphorical, allegorical, and spiritual levels (in that order), and then attained a significant refinement of the rational and imaginative faculties (in that order). All of this, in order to answer a single question with finer and finer resolution: "Where do I go from here?"

This miku-*bal* was known to have a particular skill, the ability to remove a person from his or her body, so that person might attain a more objective view of the world and its purpose. Such a teacher has many students.

One morning, after a forty-day period of deep meditation, the teacher gathered his students to announce that he was leaving the school to become the rabbi of a liberal congregation in an affluent suburb in New Jersey.

The students were shocked beyond speech.

"Anyone can do what I do here," the teacher explained.

"With students like you, it is easy. The real challenge, the real test, is to see if what I do here can be done in an affluent suburb in New Jersey."

"But rabbi," they protested, "within a few months you will be miserable. There is no one for you to learn with in that community."

"Still, I have to go. It's not my decision."

What choice did they have? They accepted their teacher's path and wished him farewell.

The teacher moved with his family to New Jersey. Within a few months he was miserable. The people in the community were not only devoid of learning and empty of prayer, but valued neither.

"Why am I here?" he asked.

"To teach," came the inner response. "Why else would you be here?"

"To teach whom?"

"That's for you to figure out."

The rabbi called the president of the congregation. "Next Sunday morning," he said, "I would like to speak to every member—every man, every woman, every child."

Never before had such a request been made. The president, eager to please his rabbi, sent out the word by mail and by phone. The next Sunday the gathering in the sanctuary was greater than the most holy of days. Every seat was taken. Additional chairs were set in the aisles, along the walls, and, even then, some were standing.

The rabbi began with a teaching, beginning with Hebrew words: *Sh'ma yis-ra-el, Adonai Elo-haynu, Adonai ehad.* "Hear, Israel, the Lord is our God, and the Lord is one." Those were the central words of Jewish teaching about God, both from the Bible and prayer.

"You are not ready to use the words *Lord* or *God* yet," he said. "So when I teach you how to chant, we'll use the sounds *la-la-la* and *la-la-la-lah* instead. Then, when we're ready, we'll use *Adonai Elohaynu*, the Lord is our God."

The community listened to the teaching, then began to chant with the rabbi. "Hear, Israel, *la-la-la, la-la-la-lah, la-la-la* is one."

The community had never chanted anything before, and the *la-la-la's* seemed silly, but they followed instruction, and after a few minutes, the chanting built in energy and began to reach an intensity the community had never before experienced. Ten minutes they chanted. Twenty. Thirty.

"Stop," said the rabbi. "Enough."

For those, both seated and standing, it was not enough. But they followed instruction and stopped.

"Enough," the rabbi repeated. "Go home. Go home."

A murmur of confusion rippled through the community,

an uneasy rustling as people stood, turned, and left.

Within a few minutes the sanctuary was empty of everyone except the rabbi and one small person, a little girl, who walked up to him and said, "What did you do that for?"

"What do you mean?"

"We were enjoying that. I was enjoying it. It was fun, more fun than anything else I've ever done here. And besides, you never let us use the name of God even once. *La-la-la, la-la-la-lah.* What's that supposed to mean?"

"It doesn't mean anything," the rabbi said. "The purpose of this isn't for you to have fun. And you aren't ready yet to use the names of God."

"What do you mean, I'm not ready?"

"Do you really want to know?"

"Yes."

"Do you *really* want to know?"

The little girl heard the *really*. Stories were told about this rabbi, that he could take a person out of the body.

"Yes," she said, surprised she had said it. "I *really* want to know."

"Then sit down right here." She sat in the front pew. "Close your eyes." She closed her eyes. "Don't forget to breathe." She had been holding her breath, as if somehow she were underwater. She opened her mouth, breathed in, breathed out. "This won't hurt." Before she had time to think about it not hurting she felt a little tug.

"You can open your eyes now."

She opened her eyes. The rabbi was standing right in front of her.

"What do you see?" he asked.

"I see you," she said. She looked around. "I see the sanctuary." She looked behind her. "And I see me sitting there in the front row." She looked at herself sitting with her eyes closed. "I'm smaller than I thought I was."

"You know," the rabbi said, "when you're out of your body like this, you don't have to stay here standing on the floor. You could go right up to the ceiling."

She looked upward and began to float toward the ceiling.

"What do you see?" the rabbi asked.

She looked down. "You, looking up at me. And me, sitting there with my eyes closed."

"You know," the rabbi said, "when you're out of your body like this, you don't have to stop at the ceiling. You can go right through the roof."

She looked upward, tested with her finger. It went through the ceiling. Her arm followed, then the rest of her, and she found herself above the trees, floating in the air.

"What do you see?" the rabbi asked.

"The parking lot." It took her a moment, but she found it. "My house." She lived only a block away. "The roof of the sanctuary." She could see the roof. "You looking up, and a tiny me sitting in front of you."

"You know," the rabbi said, "when you're out of your body like this, not only can you go up to the ceiling and through the roof, you could go higher, right up to the clouds."

She looked upward. To look was to go. She was as high as the clouds.

"What do you see?" the rabbi asked.

"New York," was the first thing she saw. "The ocean. Mountains. Down there is my house, somewhere. And a tiny, tiny me."

"You know," the rabbi said, "when you're out of your body like this, not only can you go up to the ceiling and through the roof and up to the clouds, you could go higher still, if you like, right to the edge of the atmosphere."

She looked upward. Again, to look was to go. Out she went, way beyond the clouds, to where the sky became black instead of blue. She turned around and looked down.

"What do you see?" the rabbi asked.

It was a while before she could answer. What she saw took her breath away. She reminded herself to keep breathing. "I see the curve of the earth," she whispered. "And the blue ocean and white clouds. And the mountains. And tiny cities." She couldn't find her own city. She began to tremble. "And way down there, somewhere, is a tiny, tiny me."

"You know," the rabbi said, "when you're out of your body like this, not only can you go up to the ceiling and through the roof, up to the clouds, and out to the edge of the atmosphere. If you like, you could go to the very center of the universe."

She thought about that. To think was to go. She followed her thoughts out through the solar system, by Mars, Jupiter, Saturn. Out of the solar system through the galaxy. Out of the galaxy through clusters of galaxies, to the very center of the universe.

After a long time, she heard the rabbi's voice, barely a whisper in her mind. "What do you see?"

She didn't know how to answer.

"What do you feel?"

That she knew. "I'm afraid," she said.

"Why are you afraid?"

"Because I have no idea where I am, and no idea how I'll ever get back."

"When you're ready to get back," the rabbi whispered, "ask."

"Ask whom?" But there was no answer.

The little girl floated at the center of the universe and thought she might disappear. Not knowing whom she was asking, she whispered, "Would you help me, please? I don't know where to go or how to get there."

Instantly she felt a breeze, so gentle, moving her, slowly at first, then fast, by clusters of galaxies, to her galaxy. By clusters of stars, to her star. Down through the planets by Saturn's rings and the moons of Jupiter to her own moon. Down into the atmosphere, softly through the clouds, just above the trees, feet-first through the roof, down, down into her body.

She opened her eyes, found the rabbi in front of her.

"What did you learn?" he asked.

She thought about that. "I learned how small I am, and how big the universe is."

"What else did you learn?"

"I learned how awesome the creator of such a universe must be."

"And what else?"

"I learned that as awesome as that creator must be, and as

tiny as I am, that creator still cares for me."

"Good," he said. "Now you're ready to use the name of God."

Together they sang, "*Sh'ma yis-ra-el, Adonai Elo-haynu, Adonai ehad.* Hear, Israel, the Lord is our God, and the Lord is one."

Of Praise and Patience

There was once a queen who reigned in a land of perfect harmony. Really perfect. Everything went well. There was always rain in its due season. The crops never failed. All the inhabitants worked side by side without quarrel. This harmony flowed from the queen, for she knew everything that happened in her realm, the nature of each of her subjects. She knew when to speak with strength, when to speak with kindness. She knew the land and the seas and the seasons, the winds, the currents. She knew how to measure and how to weigh.

She also knew herself, and she recognized within herself a yearning she did not know how to satisfy. Perhaps if I learn how to sing, she thought, I will learn to satisfy this yearning. So she learned how to sing. She studied for years, and finally she sang before her subjects, and all praised her singing. No matter what she sang, all praised her singing. All of her songs were surrounded by uniform praise.

Perhaps I do sing well, the queen thought. Perhaps not. But I will never be able to sing any better, because I never get honest criticism. My subjects love me too much.

Her yearning was not satisfied.

Then she thought she might be able to satisfy that yearning through dance. For many years she studied dance, and finally she danced before her subjects. All praised her dancing. No matter what she danced, all praised her dancing. All of her dances were surrounded by a uniform praise.

Perhaps I dance well, the queen thought. Perhaps not. I will never know, and I will never be able to dance any better. It does not matter whether I sing or dance. I have a realm that utters only praise and never criticism, and so I will never sing or dance again.

The queen's yearning remained unsatisfied.

After many years of thought the queen decided to become an artisan. She studied glass blowing and shaping. Her skill became very great, and at last she displayed a glass globe that seemed to fold in upon itself, cheating the laws of dimension. The appearance of the globe took one's breath away.

All who saw it praised it, and with the praise, the globe resonated and finally shattered. The subjects of the queen were taken aback. "It's all right," she reassured them. "I will make another." And she did, another more beautiful than the first. Again, all who saw it praised it, and again the globe resonated with the praise and shattered. "I will make another," said the queen. She did, and this one also suffered the fate of the first two.

Word spread throughout the realm of the wonder of the globes, their beauty and their frailty. To praise them was to destroy them. For months this was the only topic of discussion among the queen's subjects. They were perplexed and did not know what to do.

All this time the queen was busy with the shaping of her fourth globe, a fabrication of beauty beyond ordinary words. At last she announced to the people it was ready and all might come to see it, but no one came. No one dared to come. All were afraid to come. So the queen's most wonderful creation existed by itself with none to see it except the queen herself.

Into it she expressed her yearning. Day after day, she opened her heart into it, pouring the yearning her heart contained into the globe until the globe began to glow and shimmer with a light of its own. The light grew and pulsed and shifted throughout all the bands of the spectrum. The queen could relate to it, and she sensed the pulsing globe could somehow relate back to her. With that the queen held nothing back and poured all her yearning into the globe, but it was too much for the globe to contain. It shattered.

The cry that went out from the queen's palace was so great and filled with such anguish that everyone in the realm shuddered and hid. The queen had never known a loss like this. She turned into herself in mourning.

For a week the queen was in mourning. For a week the sharp fragments of the shattered globe lay untouched. No servant dared enter that room. At the end of the week of mourning, the queen herself went to remove the pieces. When she bent over, she saw to her astonishment that each shard contained some of the light of her yearning. The globe had shattered into myriad pieces, but each piece, no matter how small, no matter what shape, contained some of that light.

The queen considered what she should do. To sweep up the shards and throw them away was unthinkable. To touch them, to rearrange them, to try somehow to reassemble them was also unthinkable. She feared that should she so much as touch one of them, the delicate balance that sustained the light would be destroyed. All that would be left would be pieces of broken glass.

So the queen kept her distance and continued yearning toward the pieces of her creation, the pieces which contained her light, and over time she noticed that, with a will of their own, the pieces slowly moved toward each other and established bonds.

The queen was patient, her yearning constant. As each piece joined another, her joy increased.

Just a Miracle

There was a young prophet named Elijah who had just graduated from the school of prophets and started out on his own, traveling through the countryside, looking for opportunities to exercise his trade. He was in the miracle business.

He came through a village and found there a woman who was very unhappy. "Why are you so unhappy?" he asked.

"Because all of my friends are married, and I am not," she answered in tears.

"And how is it that a beautiful young woman like you is not married?"

"Because I'm not beautiful," she complained.

Elijah reached into his bag and found a mirror. "Look into this, and you will be beautiful."

She looked, and indeed she seemed to herself beautiful. Therefore, she was beautiful. In short order she found a man who could see her beauty, and she was married.

When she told the people of the village about Elijah and his mirror, they dismissed it. "It was just a self affirmation," they said.

The next year Elijah returned to the village, and again he

found the woman unhappy.

"Why are you so unhappy now?" he asked.

"Because I have no child. All of my friends have children, but my husband and I have no child."

Elijah reached into his bag and withdrew a small piece of parchment upon which was written a prayer. He told her to recite the prayer every morning and evening. Soon she became pregnant and had a son.

When she told the people about Elijah and the prayer, they dismissed it. "It was just a relaxation exercise," they said.

The next year Elijah returned to the village, and again he found the woman unhappy.

"Why are you so unhappy this time?" he asked.

"Because my husband was laid off from work. We have no money and nothing to eat."

"Nothing at all? Do you have anything in your refrigerator?"

"Only one jar of olive oil," she said.

Elijah instructed her to fetch all of her buckets and barrels, and to borrow buckets and barrels from all of her neighbors. When she opened the one jar of oil, it poured and poured and filled all of the buckets and barrels. She and her husband went into the olive oil business and did well.

When she told the people about Elijah and the jar of

oil, they dismissed it. "It was just a jar of compressed oil," they said.

The next year Elijah returned to the village, and again he found the woman unhappy, unhappier than ever. "What is the matter now?" Elijah asked.

"Our son is ill," the woman cried. "He is close to death."

Elijah went into the house and found the son was not only ill, indeed he had died. He stretched himself on top of the young boy. When he stood, the boy stirred and came back to life.

When the woman told the people about Elijah and her son, they dismissed it. "It was just CPR," they said.

Well, Elijah was fit to be tied. He had facilitated four perfectly good miracles, one to get her a husband, one to get her a child, one to get her a livelihood, and one to give life back to her son. All were good miracles, but the people of the village had dismissed them.

"I'm going away," he said, "and I won't be back until people appreciate a good miracle when they see one."

With that he summoned a fiery chariot out of heaven. It landed on the village green. Elijah climbed aboard, smiled at the beautiful young woman and asked, "Do you know how to see a miracle?" When she seemed confused, he winked. "You do know. Just think about it." Then, in sight of everyone, the chariot leaped into the sky.

Now, what do you think the people of the village said when they saw that? Did they think it was a miracle? No. They said, "It was just a special effect."

For years, the young woman thought and thought about Elijah's words. She had no idea how to see a miracle until, one day, it just popped into her head. What had Elijah said? "*Just* think about it." It wasn't the thinking. It was the word *just*! As soon as she grasped that, she was able to see miracles *just* everywhere.

She became very wise. "The word *just* puts blinders on you," she taught, "so even though a miracle might be right there in front of you, you won't be able to see it. You would see *just* this, or *just* that, but never look into the depth of anything. Your eyes would never open in wonder.

"That you open your eyes at all is a miracle. The word *just* can't keep your eyes from seeing, but the word *just* can keep you from seeing the miracle of sight.

"Every time you hear the word *just*, know that a miracle is on the other side of it. Anytime someone tells you to '*just* do something,' know they are asking for the miraculous. Don't feel so bad about not being able to accomplish it right away."

More and more students came to learn with her. Every now and then Elijah himself stopped by to listen, but she was the only one who recognized him.

The Measure of Success

No need for clergy, the son organized the service. He had only a few words to say. He had planned to say more, but found it too difficult with the unexpected presence of three such men. A conductor, an architect, a spiritual teacher. Each face had graced the covers of national magazines.

The grandchildren felt no inhibitions. They read passages precious to them, spoke their memories. Older adults found it difficult to focus, their attention wandering from the grandchildren to the three men and back again.

All stayed to see the grave covered, then turned for home. Friends had set a buffet, refreshment for the living after an encounter with death. The son invited the three to join them. He did not know why they had come, but hoped they might share that over lunch.

The mourners at the graveside service had buried a body but opened a treasure chest of shared experience. The three men sat quietly attentive while friends and family spoke. Stories emerged like pearls, one by one, until there were enough to make a necklace of memories.

The three sat together at the edge of the room, not talking

even to each other. Family members and friends of the deceased passed by them on their way out, muttered a few words and shook hands. Such was their fleeting encounter with greatness.

At last there remained only the immediate family, the three men, and still too much food on the table.

"You've had something to eat?" the son asked, addressing no one in particular.

"I'm not hungry, thank you," the conductor said. The others nodded in agreement.

The great-grandchildren had retreated to play. The remainder of the family circled chairs around, sat with the three men, waited for them to speak.

"I met your father once," the conductor began.

"Me, too," said the architect. "Just once."

"I, also," the teacher said. "Once."

"He never spoke of it," the son said. "Did you meet with him all together?"

"As for me, I was alone with him," the teacher said, looking toward the other two.

"Alone, also," said the architect.

"Just the two of us," said the conductor.

"He never spoke of it," the son repeated.

"I'm not surprised," the conductor said.

"It would not be his style," said the architect.

The teacher said, "I would have expected nothing else."

"You each met him only once. Something must have happened, that each of you should come so far out of your way to attend his funeral."

"Something happened." "An important moment." "A lasting impression." The three men voiced such thoughts, the words falling upon each other, but the intent clearly understandable.

"If you would be kind enough to share, we would like to hear," the son said.

"Yes," said the conductor. "Your father was a remarkable man. You must know that."

"I know him as my father," was all the son could say.

"I was with him just that once, in Central Park, on a bench. For twenty years I had removed myself from public sight. You know that? It was at the end of those twenty years I sat next to your father. He began our conversation like this:

" 'I've heard some people have such talent they can just look at a score and hear music. It's hard for me to imagine such a thing. I can't do it. The music inside them must be perfect, a perfection beyond anything they might actually bring into the world.'

"It was as if he had looked into the deepest part of my

soul and spoken a truth I had never been able to articulate. I acknowledged it, spoke of the pain I had felt in my last years of conducting and performing—that I had never once been able to bring to life the perfection I knew, and so had withdrawn into the music of my mind.

"He allowed some silence, then began with the words 'What if.'

"Such powerful words. I will never forget them. 'What if,' he said, 'you might find still more beauty in imperfection, the wrestling and sharpening of one instrument, sometimes with, sometimes against the other. A work in progress rather than a finished result. A process rather than a product. It would not be perfect any more than the image of a running stream is perfect. A stream is always moving, never stopping, never reaching a single moment of perfection. Its movement is a rush toward its perfection, never quite achieved. But the joy is in the movement, in the rush, always in progress.'

"Not his words exactly, and the conversation was longer. But that's how I've come to remember it. I returned to orchestral work shortly after, with greater joy than I had ever experienced before."

"Same here," said the architect. "If not word for word, concept for concept. I had withdrawn from my profession. I had every award under the sun. There was no goal left toward which to aspire. And the work I had done left me cold, because each building had been more beautiful in the blueprint of my mind than in the reality. In the blueprint, each work was exact, precise. In reality, each was marred by its setting, and less than perfect in the execution.

"I had enough success, enough money, nothing left for which to work. So I withdrew and sat one day on a bench in Central Park, next to your father.

"He began with just those words: 'What if. What if you gathered other architects around you to create a setting, not in the image of one alone, but one playing off the other, changing his or her design to reflect and enhance the creativity of the other, so the result would not be individual buildings, but ever changing neighborhoods to enhance ongoing life rather than isolated moments of awe?'

"Not exactly those words, but that was the sense. Soon after, I gathered a circle of associates. The result is the neighborhoods we have created in recent years."

Everyone turned to the teacher whose books had once sold in the millions, practical guides to daily living.

"I had no choice but to write," he said, "for I had the talent to see through knots in the spiritual sense, the places where people had tied themselves up in contradictions. Like a musical score to the conductor, like a blueprint to the architect, the patterns of a soul were available to me. So I wrote those books to help others free themselves from self-imposed bondage, but, over and over again, I saw them use my words to enhance their selves, to imagine they had climbed spiritual mountains, while burying themselves in the troughs of ego. So I withdrew from the world of interaction with others, seeking only inter-action with the divine. Then, some years later, I happened to sit by your father on a bench in Central Park.

"He didn't begin with the words, 'What if.' He began with, 'I can only imagine.'

" 'I can only imagine,' he said, 'what it must be like to be accosted everywhere. Such an imposition. Strangers either demanding to know some great truth, or, perhaps, attempting to thrust their truth upon you.'

"It was my situation exactly. So he took care not to address his words to me, but spoke to the air in front of him, likely knowing that if he had turned toward me, I would have run away.

"Your father's talent was greater than mine. He saw the pattern of my soul, and how to . . . encounter it . . . how to encounter it in such a way as to make the moment sacred. I had a sense of his holiness, and so stayed on the bench beside him.

"Then he said, 'What if. What if instead of teaching one's own insights, one learned the texts of others? Such a person might attract a circle of students willing to learn. Then the energy in the room might move around the circle, rather than be directed from teacher to student.'

"I heard his words, but didn't understand him. I told him it was my custom to teach from my heart. I wasn't an academic teacher. I didn't know enough of the spiritual texts to create a curriculum and teach with authority. I didn't want to teach a class, being just a day ahead of my students.

"I had misunderstood him entirely. He hadn't suggested that I teach. He had suggested that I learn.

" 'Learning,' he said, 'is not teaching. It would not be your task to be a day ahead of anybody, but rather to be as ignorant as everybody around the table. Should you profess ignorance, you would have nothing to lose, for no one would expect anything of you. By not filling space with your own teaching, you would invite the participation of others. The interaction of one intellect against the other, one soul with the other, would sharpen and polish not only the individuals, but the group as a whole.'

"Those were not his exact words, rather a description of what I have enjoyed these last years, with a circle of learners. And so my recent work hasn't come from me at all, but rather from us. I have been able to find my way, bit by bit, back into the world."

Together they sat some time in silence, the three men looking to the family, the family to them.

"What of you?" the architect asked the son. "We each had but a single encounter with your father, and each encounter was indeed a sacred moment. You grew up with him. Was there any particular encounter you might share with us, something that redirected your life?"

"I knew him as my father," the son said, not knowing how else to respond.

The conductor said, "Forgive me, please. I came to the funeral to honor your father, but I came to your home out of curiosity. It isn't for me to put pressure on you at a time like this."

"No pressure," said the son. "I really don't know how to answer. You each had these great encounters, but then each of you is a great man. You've accomplished extraordinary things. I'm just a son who had a father."

The son began to cry, struggled to control his tears.

"Not to worry," the teacher said. "This isn't fair. I suspect we each came hoping for another taste. We shouldn't be asking this of you."

Eyes closed, the son waved the words away to make room for his own. "I'm crying because I do remember. One occasion comes to mind." He opened his eyes, looked to each of the great men in turn. "A simple moment, not as profound as yours. I was twelve years old. I had just returned from summer camp. On the doorway of the kitchen we kept a record of my height. I had measured myself just before leaving for camp, and then made a mark above that, the amount I intended to grow in my time away. When I returned at the end of the summer, I measured myself against the kitchen door and found myself a half-inch below the mark I had set for myself.

"My father saw how disappointed I was. I told him I had failed. I hadn't grown enough.

"At first he didn't say anything. He looked at the mark I had made. With his thumb he smudged it out, took a pencil, and marked my real growth. Then he spoke. 'You've grown wonderfully well,' he said. 'Your only failure was that you made your mark too high.'

"Those were his exact words.

"Now every time I reach too high and fail, I adjust the mark. Then, from that platform of success, I am able to reach still higher."

The three great men stayed a while longer. When they left, each had words of comfort and appreciation.

Epilogue

Our Wall Street man paused after the first story, *The Curse of Blessings*. His worldview has shifted. He said he would digest what he had learned and return to the other stories later. That was some months ago. *The Curse of Blessings* is still working within him.

Our social worker smiled at the first story, and the second. Each brought its own satisfaction, and then *Polished Stones*. That's where she stopped reading, for the woes of the world had been wearing her down. She's developing a new way of regarding those moments where her own life seems to have gone astray. She has much to consider before reading on.

Our diamond merchant read quickly from one story to the next. He saw in each just where the story was going, though the endings sometimes took him by surprise. Still, they were just stories. Then he read *Just a Miracle*. He's gone back to the beginning to read again what he had thought to be *just* stories.

As for me, I read all the way through, pausing after each story to savor it. I thought all the stories were the same, each with a different flavor. However, none of the flavors were quite mine. So I picked up a pen and began to write, first the introduction to this collection, then words of my own.

I can only hope that when my stories are done, they find their readers, just as Reuben's stories found us—and when I say "us," I include you. Thanks for joining our story circle. May *The Curse of Blessings* work its blessings within you.

Afterthoughts

These stories are from my imagination. I have a Jewish-flavored imagination. However, if one dives below the particular words, one finds an original source from which all stories come.

Some of the stories in this volume have appeared before in novels. *The Curse of Blessings* is drawn directly from *The Seventh Telling: The Kabbalah of Moshe Katan* (St. Martin's Press, 2001). *The Miku-bal in New Jersey* and *Just a Miracle* are adapted from the same novel, *Of Praise and Patience* is drawn from the sequel, *The Thirty-Third Hour* (St. Martin's Press, 2002).

Mouth of the Mountain emanates from a teaching of the Focolare, a community of the Catholic Church. That, too, comes from my Jewish experience. As a teacher of Jewish spirituality I interact with and am influenced by teachers of other spiritual traditions, in this instance Father Joseph Sievers.

Joseph Buchwald Gelles was the first to suggest publication of the stories apart from the novels. That suggestion, relayed through my agent Natasha Kern, resulted in this happy collaboration with Deborah Grandinetti, Jon Anderson, and Rick Joyce at Running Press.

My wife, Walli, and my three sons have helped with all of my projects, reading and responding with compassionate honesty. This volume is dedicated to the three boys, all three at once, there being no guarantee I will have additional books to honor each in turn—so I took care to shape the dedication in such a way that I could list each one first.

And, lastly, thank *you*. You've had such faith to read this far!

If you like, you can reach me through my Web Site, www.mitchellchefitz.com.

Love and blessings
—Mitch